TIME
FOR KIDS
READERS

W9-BEH-893

UNITED STATES MINT

THE
Mint

by Susan Ring

Harcourt

Orlando   Austin   Chicago   New York   Toronto   London   San Diego

Visit *The Learning Site!*
www.harcourtschool.com

These are new state quarters. Soon there will be one quarter for each state. Where do these quarters come from?

Has your state's quarter been made yet?

The quarters all come from the United States Mint. That is where nickels, dimes, and quarters are made.

The United States Mint in Denver, Colorado, makes many coins.

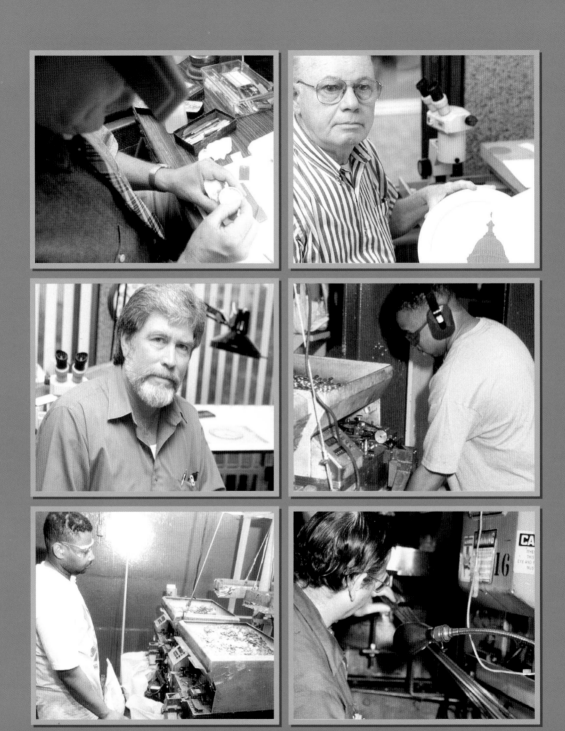

Many people work at the Mint. Each person has a different job to do. It takes many steps to make a coin.

All coins begin as sheets of metal.

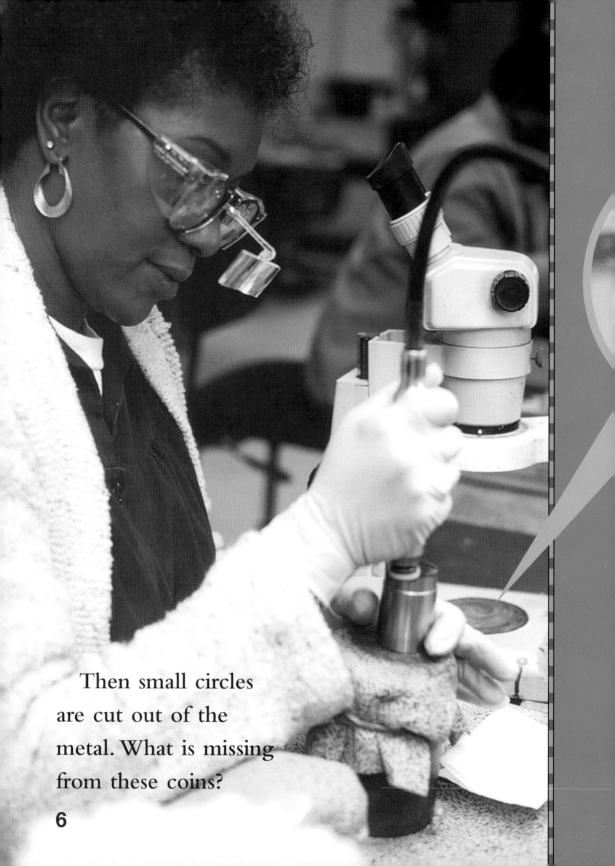

Then small circles
are cut out of the
metal. What is missing
from these coins?

There are no pictures on them yet. Next, words and pictures are stamped on both sides. Then people look at the coins very carefully. Each coin must be exactly the right size and shape.

The coins are put into large bags. They are ready to go to the bank. Guards take the coins to the bank. From there, the coins will go to you.

Now you know where those quarters came from. They were made at the Mint.